BR
35 05/1

EXPLORING THE HUMAN BODY

The Stomach and Digestion

Carol Ballard

FRANKLIN WATTS
LONDON•SYDNEY

First published in 2005 by
Franklin Watts
96 Leonard Street
London EC2A 4XD

Franklin Watts Australia
Level 17/207 Kent Street
Sydney
NSW 2000

Produced by Arcturus Publishing Ltd,
26/27 Bickels Yard, 151–153 Bermondsey Street, London SE1 3HA

Series concept: Alex Woolf
Editor: Alex Woolf
Designer: Peta Morey
Artwork: Michael Courtney
Picture researcher: Glass Onion Pictures
Consultant: Dr Kristina Routh

Picture Credits
Science Photo Library: 5 (Bluestone), 7 (Lauren Shear), 9 (Mark Clarke),
11 (BSIP, Laurent), 13 (Eye of Science), 15 (Eye of Science), 17 (Coneyl Jay),
19 (Ian Boddy), 20 (Maximilian Stock Ltd), 21 (Mark Clarke), 22 (Ricardo Arias,
Latin Stock), 24 (Jason Kelvin), 25 (BSIP, Chassenet), 26 (Jim Gipe/Agstock),
27 (Adrienne Hart-Davis), 28 (Adam Hart-Davis), 29 (Bluestone).

Every attempt has been made to clear copyright. Should there be any
inadvertent omission, please apply to the publisher for rectification.

A CIP catalogue record for this book is available from the British Library

ISBN 0 7496 5967 X

Printed in Singapore

Contents

What is Digestion?

Your food provides everything you need to be active, to grow and to stay healthy. Your body cannot use the food just as it is – it has to break it down into all the different substances that it contains. This breaking-down process is called digestion.

Your body is made up of many different organs, each with its own special job to do. Digestion is carried out by the organs of your digestive system. This is really just a tube nearly nine metres long, that goes from your mouth to your anus. Some of the organs are curled up so that it can all fit inside you! The organs all work together to break down your food so that the substances it contains are released.

Digestion begins in your mouth when you take a mouthful of food and chew it. When you swallow, the chewed-up food passes into the foodpipe, or oesophagus. From there, it moves into the stomach. It passes into the small intestine and on into the large intestine. When there are no useful substances left, the waste leaves your body when you go to the toilet.

This picture shows how your digestive system is organized inside your body.

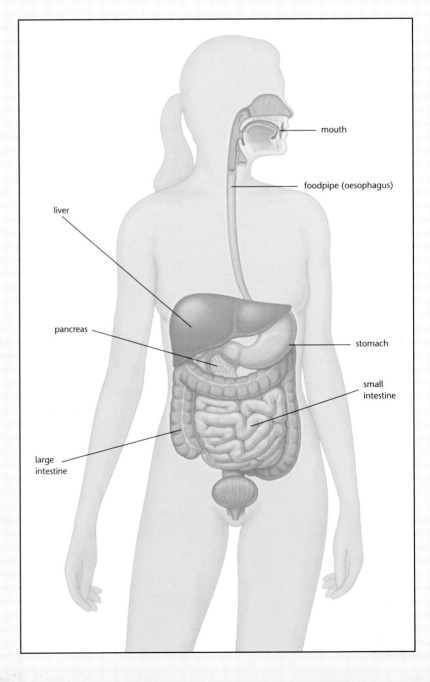

mouth

foodpipe (oesophagus)

liver

pancreas

stomach

small intestine

large intestine

Other organs are involved in the process too. Although they are not actually part of the digestive system, they carry out essential jobs that are related to digestion. Without your liver, pancreas, kidneys and bladder, the process of digestion would not work properly.

Different foods contain different substances. Some contain a lot of useful substances, so they are good for your body. Others contain few useful substances and may even contain substances that can make you unhealthy, so they are not good for your body. Knowing what is in different foods, and choosing those that are good for you, can help you to stay healthy.

Which fruits would you choose for a delicious, healthy snack?

How much you eat can affect your health. Eating too much or too little is not good for you and can make you unhealthy. Drinks are important too. Your body needs plenty of water to stay healthy, especially when the weather is hot or when you have been very active.

Case notes

Why do we need food?

Food provides your body with the substances it needs for:

1. Energy for activity: even when you are asleep, your body is using energy as you breathe, your heart beats and your brain dreams.
2. Making new skin, bone, muscle and other things: your body needs to be able to do this so that you can grow, and repair damage like a cut knee or broken arm.
3. Staying healthy: to help it fight infections and resist disease, your body needs special substances from food.

Teeth

Without teeth, many ordinary foods would be very difficult to eat! We use our teeth to bite into our food, to tear sticky food and to chew chunks of food. Each of these jobs is done by different teeth.

Incisor teeth are at the front of your mouth. These have sharp edges for biting into your food. Canine teeth are the pointed teeth at each side of the incisors. They are good for piercing, gripping and tearing food. Premolar teeth are behind the canines. They have blunt, broad surfaces for crushing food. Molar teeth are at the back of your mouth. Their large, bumpy surfaces are ideal for chewing, mashing and grinding food.

You only see part of each tooth (the crown), because the rest (the root) is stuck firmly inside your jawbone. Teeth are made up from several layers: a hard, shiny outer layer called enamel, an inner hard layer called dentine and a soft centre called pulp that contains nerves and blood vessels.

This diagram shows the layers that make up a tooth.

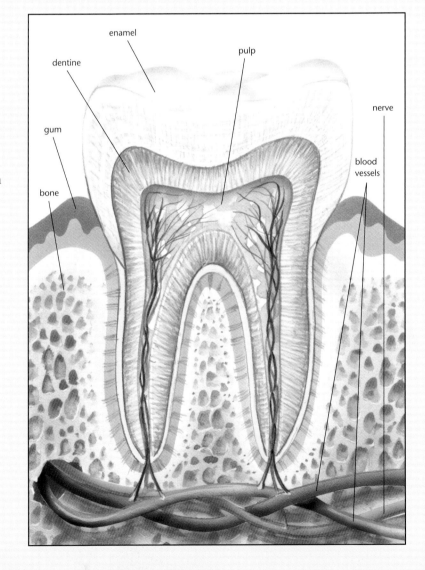

enamel

pulp

dentine

nerve

gum

blood vessels

bone

Babies are born without any teeth. By the time they are about a year old, they have a set of twenty "milk teeth". Between about six and twelve years old, the milk teeth fall out one by one, and are replaced by a set of permanent teeth. There are thirty-two teeth in a full adult set: eight incisors, four canines, eight premolars and twelve molars. The final four molars, called wisdom teeth, do not usually appear until several years after the other molars, and sometimes do not appear at all.

Here you can see the different types of front teeth – incisors in the centre, then the pointed canine and premolar (right).

It is important to look after your teeth. Brushing them every morning and evening is a good start. Dental floss can also help to get rid of any food scraps that are stuck between your teeth. Try to avoid eating too many sweets and sugary drinks, especially between meals when the sugar will remain in your mouth for a long time. Regular visits to your dentist will allow any damage and other problems to be detected early, when they can easily be put right.

Case notes

What causes tooth decay?

Tooth decay is caused by micro-organisms called bacteria that live in your mouth. If they have a supply of sugar, they can grow and multiply. They make a thin white film called plaque that sticks to your teeth. Bacteria also produce acid that slowly dissolves the tooth, making a hole in it. Unless the damage is repaired by a dentist, the acid will dissolve more and more of the tooth and eventually reach the nerve. This can be extremely painful!

Mouth

When you take a bite of food, it goes into your mouth. Your teeth chew it, crushing and mashing it into small, soft pieces. It is mixed with a liquid called saliva that is made by special glands under your tongue and in the sides of your mouth. Saliva helps to soften the food and begins the process of digestion. It also makes food moist and slippery so that it is easy to swallow.

Your tongue moves your food around inside your mouth. The top surface of your tongue contains clusters of special taste-sensitive cells called taste buds. When food touches these, they send signals to your brain. Your nose also sends signals to the brain about what the food smells like. Your brain interprets these and works out what you are tasting.

This diagram shows the structures that make up your nose and mouth.

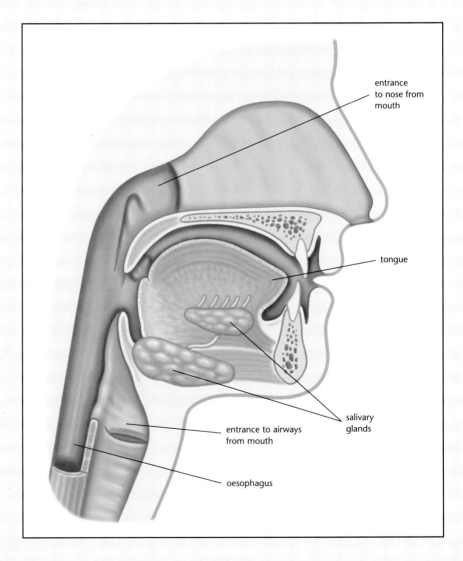

entrance to nose from mouth

tongue

salivary glands

entrance to airways from mouth

oesophagus

Which flavours do you like best?

Although there are many different flavours in your food, there are only four main tastes – sweet, salty, bitter and sour. Mixing these four tastes together in different ways creates the full range of different flavours that we enjoy in our food.

When your food is soft and moist, it is ready to swallow. A flap blocks off the windpipe to stop food going into the airways. The soft palate blocks off the entrance to the nose. Your tongue pushes the food to the back of your mouth. When it touches the back of your mouth, an automatic reaction forces it out of the mouth and into the foodpipe, or oesophagus.

The oesophagus is a tube that connects your mouth and stomach. It has strong muscular walls. The muscles contract and relax in waves, forcing the food along it towards the stomach. Most of the time a ring of muscle keeps the entrance to the stomach closed. When food reaches it, the ring of muscle relaxes, opening the stomach entrance to let the food through.

Case notes

What happens when I vomit?

Sometimes you have to get rid of whatever is in your stomach. This might be because you've eaten too much, or because there is something wrong with what you have eaten. Just being unwell can also make you need to empty your stomach.

To do this, the ring of muscle at the top of the stomach relaxes, and the stomach muscles force food out into the oesophagus. The oesophagus muscles work in reverse, pushing the food backwards and out through the mouth. We call this process being sick, or vomiting. The vomit tastes unpleasant because the food has been mixed with acid and other juices in your stomach.

Stomach

Your stomach is at the end of your oesophagus, just below your ribs. An adult's stomach is about 25 centimetres long, and a child's is a little smaller. It is rather like a balloon with stretchy walls and a space inside. The walls are made of strong, elastic muscles and the inside surface is very wrinkly. When the muscle walls stretch, the wrinkles are smoothed out and the space inside becomes big enough to fit a whole meal in!

The stomach walls are made up of several layers: a protective outer layer, muscle layers, and an inside lining. The inside lining of the stomach contains special gastric glands. These make a liquid called gastric juice which plays an important part in digesting food. Gastric juice is a mixture of different things:

- enzymes: chemicals that break the food down into smaller pieces;
- hydrochloric acid: a substance that kills micro-organisms, dissolves minerals and helps the enzymes to work;
- mucus: a slimy liquid that lubricates the food and forms a layer over the inside of the stomach to protect it from the gastric juice.

This diagram shows what your stomach is like inside.

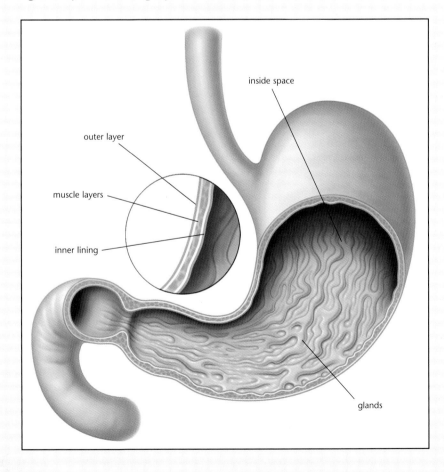

inside space

outer layer

muscle layers

inner lining

glands

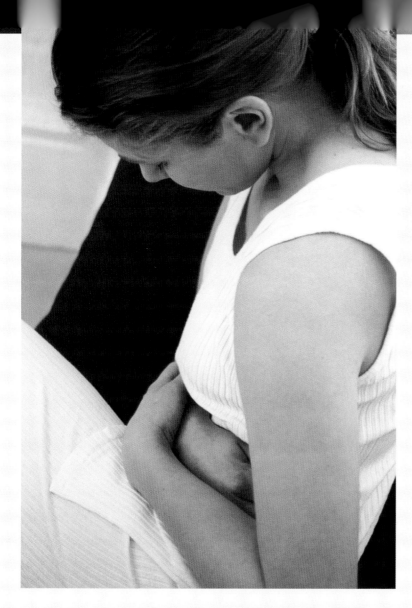

You may feel uncomfortable after a big meal, but a quiet rest will often help you to feel better.

When food enters the stomach, the muscles of the stomach wall begin to contract and relax. These movements churn the food around so that it mixes with the gastric juices. Slowly, the food is turned into a thick liquid called chyme. When the chyme is ready to leave the stomach, a ring of muscle at the lower end opens. Chyme is squirted out of the stomach and into the next part of the digestive system, the small intestine.

Some foods stay in the stomach longer than others, because they take longer to break down into chyme. Water passes through very quickly, in just a few minutes. Foods like white bread, rice, potatoes and pasta may stay in the stomach for about an hour. The slowest foods, such as chips, sausages and other meats, may take several hours to pass through.

Case notes

What causes indigestion?

Sometimes, after a meal, people have a tummy ache or they feel sick, or they may get a burning sensation above the stomach. This is often because they have indigestion. Several things can cause this:

- some types of food
- eating too much
- eating too quickly
- stress

Indigestion may be uncomfortable but it soon passes and it is not dangerous. Resting quietly for a while often helps. To avoid indigestion, try eating more slowly, and perhaps have smaller, more frequent meals.

Small Intestine

The small intestine is actually the longest part of the digestive system – if it was fully stretched out, it would be more than six metres long! It is called "small" because for most of its length it is a very narrow tube. It is coiled up tightly so that it can fit inside your abdomen.

There are three main parts to the small intestine. The first part, just below the stomach, is called the duodenum. Here, more digestive juices are added to the chyme. A yellowy-green liquid called bile, which is made in the liver, helps to break up fats into small droplets. Pancreatic juice from the pancreas contains some enzymes to break down the other chemicals in the chyme. It also contains a substance to make the chyme less acidic.

The jejunum is the middle part of the small intestine, and the final part is the ileum. The walls of the small intestine are made up of layers in the same way as the stomach walls. The muscle layers help to move the food along the small intestine by contracting and relaxing in a wave movement. The inner lining contains glands that make thin mucus to help the food slide along smoothly. Some digestive juices are made here also, to complete the process of digestion.

Digestive enzymes break food up into smaller units that your body can use.

smaller chains

large nutrient chain

enzymes act like scissors

separate units

Once the food has been completely broken down, the nutrients have to get to the parts of the body where they are needed. The inner lining of the small intestine is folded up and has millions of tiny finger-like tufts called villi. These have very thin walls so that nutrients can easily pass into them. The villi have blood vessels inside them, so nutrients can pass into the blood and be carried away to other parts of the body. Some water is also absorbed from the food by the small intestine.

This photograph was taken looking down a microscope. You can see the villi of the intestinal wall.

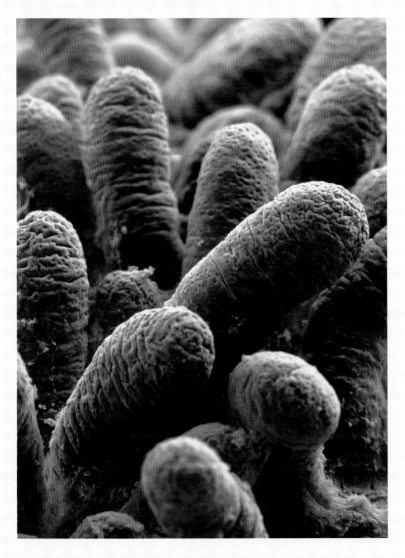

By the time it reaches the end of the small intestine, the food has been completely digested and all the nutrients have been taken out. All that is left of the food is waste material that your body cannot use.

Case notes

Why can't some people drink milk?

Milk contains a type of sugar called lactose. This is usually broken down in the small intestine by a special enzyme called lactase. In some people, the small intestine does not produce enough lactase so the lactose cannot be broken down. It stays in the waste, causing diarrhoea, wind and cramps. This condition is known as "lactose intolerance". Most people who suffer from this avoid drinking milk and eating foods made from milk such as cheese and yoghurt.

Large Intestine

What is left of the food after it has moved through the small intestine passes on into the large intestine. This is only about one sixth of the length of the small intestine, but it is much wider. It bends round to make a rectangular shape around the small intestine. Its walls are made up of layers, just as in the stomach and small intestine.

The first part of the large intestine is called the caecum. This is very short, and really just joins the small and large intestines together. Attached to the caecum is a long, thin pouch called the appendix, which does not seem to have any important digestive function in humans.

The main part of the large intestine is called the colon. The muscles in the colon walls contract and relax in waves to push the waste along. Special cells in the colon walls produce mucus to help the waste slide along easily. Water from the waste is absorbed by the colon walls, so the waste slowly becomes drier and more solid.

This diagram shows the shape of your large intestine.

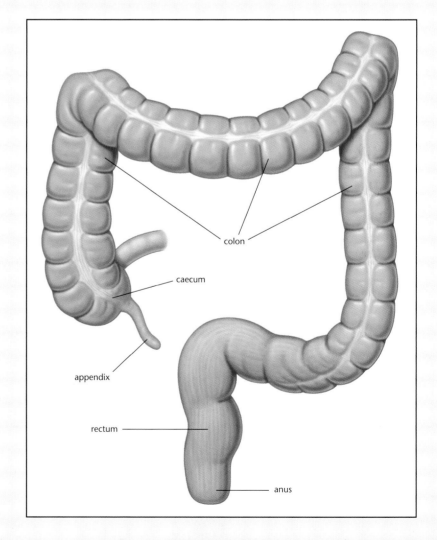

colon

caecum

appendix

rectum

anus

The final part of the large intestine is called the rectum. Solid waste material, called faeces, can be stored here for several hours. Eventually, when the rectum becomes full, you feel you need to go to the toilet. Babies and very young children cannot stop themselves from getting rid of faeces when their rectums are full. As you grow, you learn to control a ring of muscle, called the anus, around the end of the rectum. When this opens, faeces passes through and leaves your body.

The colon contains millions of harmless bacteria that help to finish breaking down the waste material. As they do this, they release a mixture of gases. If a lot of gas is produced, you may need to get rid of it by breaking wind. The bacteria play an important part in completing the digestive process. Some people eat foods such as "live" yoghurts that contain lots of these bacteria, to keep their digestive systems working well.

Faeces contains bacteria and other germs. To avoid spreading these to other places and other people, and to keep yourself clean and healthy, you should always wash your hands after using the toilet.

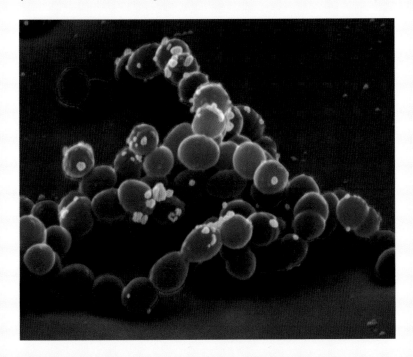

Look at the bacteria that can grow if you do not wash your hands!

Case notes

How long does food stay in the intestines?

Normally, it takes between six and fifteen hours for food to pass right through the intestines. If you have eaten some food that has gone bad, something to which you are allergic, or something that is poisonous, your body will need to get rid of it quickly. The food will rush through the intestines much faster than normal. We call this diarrhoea. There will not be enough time for water to be absorbed, so when you go to the toilet, the waste will be much softer than usual. Constipation is the opposite of diarrhoea – food stays in the intestines for longer than normal, so more water is absorbed and the waste becomes dry and hard.

Liver and Pancreas

Food does not actually pass through the liver or pancreas, so they are not really organs of the digestive system. Without them, though, you would not be able to digest your food properly.

The liver is a large organ made up of two parts called lobes. It lies mostly on the right side of your body, just below the ribs. The liver is like an amazing chemical factory, carrying out lots of jobs. It helps to control the amount of sugar in your blood and converts excess sugar to fat. It helps break down old blood cells and stores any useful chemicals they contain. It also removes harmful chemicals like poisons and drugs from your blood.

Carrying out these processes produces heat, and this warms the blood as it flows through the liver. As the blood travels around the rest of the body, the heat it picked up from the liver helps to keep you warm.

One of the liver's important jobs is to produce a yellow-green liquid called bile. This is stored in a small pouch called the gall bladder, which is tucked in between the lobes of the liver. The gall bladder releases bile into the small intestine, where it breaks down fats. Without bile, your body would not be able to digest fats properly.

Here you can see how the liver, gall bladder and pancreas fit around some of the organs of the digestive system.

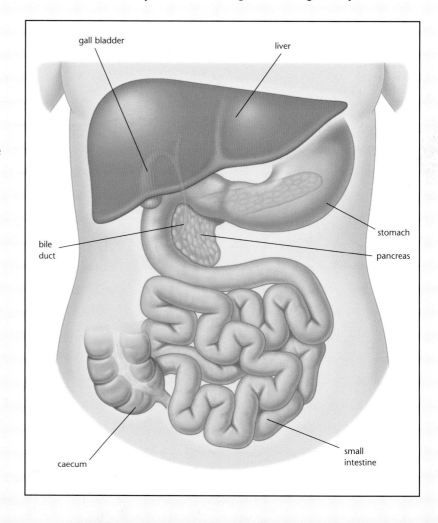

gall bladder

liver

bile duct

stomach

pancreas

caecum

small intestine

This girl has diabetes and needs regular injections of insulin.

The pancreas is a small organ that lies just behind the stomach. It produces pancreatic juice and releases it into the small intestine. Pancreatic juice contains enzymes that help to digest food. The pancreas also produces insulin and glucagon, two special chemicals that help to control the amount of sugar in the blood.

The liver and pancreas work together to make sure there is exactly the right amount of sugar in the blood. If there is not enough, the pancreas produces extra glucagon. This makes the liver release sugar into the blood. If there is too much sugar in the blood, the pancreas produces extra insulin. One of the effects of this is to make the liver take sugar out of the blood and store it.

Case notes

What is diabetes?

A person with diabetes cannot control the amount of sugar in their blood properly. This may be because their pancreas does not produce enough insulin, or it may be because their body cannot use the insulin properly. Some people can control their diabetes by eating a low-sugar diet, exercising regularly and making sure they are not overweight. Others need to inject themselves regularly with insulin.

Kidneys and Bladder

Your blood collects water and nutrients from the intestines. It also collects waste products from every part of your body. Anything that your body cannot use has to be removed from your blood, or else your organs cannot work properly and you will be ill. Making sure that your blood contains exactly the right amounts of water, sugar and salts is the job of your kidneys.

You have two kidneys, one on either side of your spine. Each is about ten centimetres long, with a dent in one side as if it has been squeezed. Inside a kidney are millions of tiny tubes called nephrons.

When blood reaches the kidneys, it is full of waste materials that need to be removed. As blood travels around the nephrons, some water, salts, minerals and other chemicals are filtered out. Clean blood leaves the kidneys and travels back around to other parts of the body.

The water and waste materials that were filtered out of the blood are collected together in the centre of the kidney, making the liquid we call urine. This leaves the kidney via a tube called a ureter, which takes it to the bladder.

Here you can see where the kidneys and bladder are in the body.

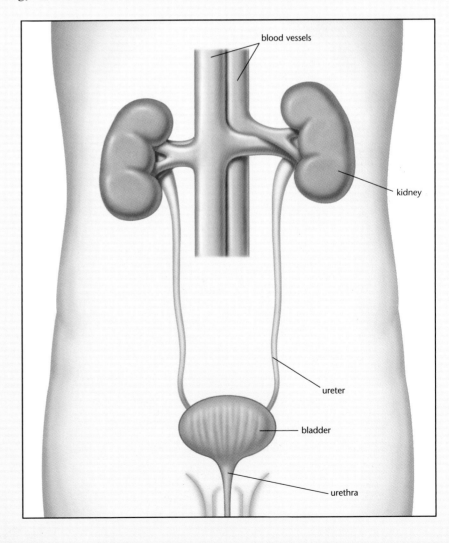

blood vessels

kidney

ureter

bladder

urethra

The bladder is a stretchy bag that slowly fills up with urine from the kidneys. It can hold more than half a litre of urine! When it is nearly full, it sends signals to your brain and you know you need to empty your bladder. Urine leaves your body via a tube called the urethra. A ring of muscle in the urethra allows you to control when you go to the toilet.

Washing your hands after using the toilet gets rid of harmful germs that you may have picked up there.

Normally, each person produces more than a litre of urine every day. If you drink a lot, more urine will be produced because there is more liquid to get rid of. If you sweat a lot, less urine will be produced because some water will be lost as sweat.

You can be perfectly healthy with just one kidney, but would be very ill if both kidneys stopped working properly. People whose kidneys do not work properly can have their blood cleaned by a dialysis machine. This often involves long visits to hospital several times every week. Some patients are able to have a kidney transplant – one of their sick kidneys is removed and replaced with a kidney from another person.

Case notes

Why is urine yellow?

Urine is mainly water, with a lot of chemicals dissolved in it. It gets its yellowish colour from a chemical called bilirubin. This is released when old blood cells are broken down by the liver. Bilirubin leaves the liver as part of the bile and enters the digestive system. From there, it moves into the bloodstream. It is removed from the blood by the kidneys and ends up in your urine. The more bilirubin there is in your urine, the darker the colour will be.

A Balanced Diet

Your diet is everything you eat and drink. It should provide your body with all the nutrients needed for being active, growing and staying healthy. Different types of food provide different nutrients, but no food provides everything. It makes sense to eat a range of foods to provide your body with a mixture of nutrients. A diet that contains all the nutrients you need is called a balanced diet. There are four main groups of nutrients:

● proteins
● vitamins and minerals
● carbohydrates
● fats

Can you match each type of food to the nutrients it provides?

Make sure you drink plenty of water, especially when you're busy!

If you look at packets and tins of food, you can usually see a panel that says "Nutrition Information". This gives you details about the nutrients that the food contains. It can help you to make healthy choices about what you eat.

To stay healthy, it is also important to drink plenty of water, to keep your kidneys working well. This is especially important in hot weather and when you are taking part in sports activities.

The food that you eat gives you energy. When you are active, you use energy. To stay healthy, you need to balance the amount you eat with the amount of activity you do.

If you eat more than your body needs, your body will store the extra as fat. This will make it harder for you to do everyday things like run and play. People who are extremely fat are described as obese. This can be very bad for their health and they can become quite ill.

If you eat less than your body needs, your body will use up all of its fat stores. This will make your body weaker and you might feel too tired to be active. Being too thin can be just as bad for your health as being too fat.

Case notes

What is anorexia?

Some people can be very unhappy about the way they look, and think they are much too fat. They may stop eating properly. They eat less and less and become very thin. This makes them weak and ill, but they still refuse to eat. People who do this are said to have anorexia. Anorexia is so dangerous that some people die from it.

Proteins

Proteins are found in foods such as meats, fish, eggs and nuts. These foods are often the main part of a meal, with other things added – for example, we talk about fish and chips, chicken curry, and bacon sandwiches. The fish, chicken and bacon are the protein foods and they form the main part of each meal. The chips, curry and sandwich bread make up the rest of each meal.

Foods made from milk are also good sources of protein. These include milk, cheese and yoghurt. Some doctors feel that, because dairy products also contain fats, you should not eat very much of them. An alternative is to choose low-fat or fat-free products. Other doctors think that, unless you are very overweight, eating dairy products as part of a balanced diet is good for you.

The meats in this picture are all good sources of protein.

Proteins are the building blocks for your body. They help you to grow strong and to repair damage such as cut skin and broken bones. If there is not enough protein in your diet, your body will not be strong and healthy.

It is a good idea to try to eat at least two portions of protein-rich food every day.

Proteins are made from simpler chemicals called amino acids, strung together rather like beads on a necklace. When proteins are digested, the amino acids are separated. Your body can then rearrange the amino acids in different orders to make all the different proteins that it needs.

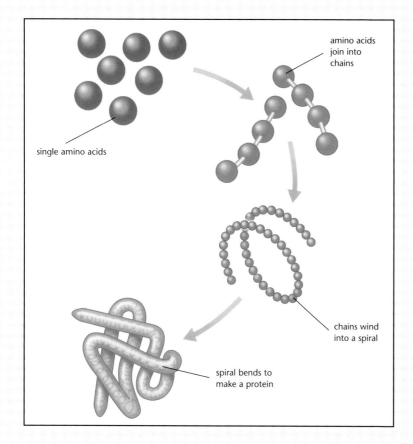

amino acids join into chains

single amino acids

chains wind into a spiral

spiral bends to make a protein

This picture shows how amino acids are put together to make a protein.

Many people are vegetarians, which means that they do not eat meat. This may be because they think it is wrong to use animals for food, for religious reasons, or simply because they do not like meat.

Some vegetarians do not eat fish either, and vegans do not eat any animal products at all. They have to get their proteins from other foods. Foods such as nuts, lentils and chickpeas are good non-animal sources of proteins. Soya beans contain a lot of protein and can be used in a wide variety of dishes instead of meat. Some mushroom-like plants can be used to make protein-rich foods too.

Case notes

What if I'm vegetarian?

Being vegetarian is fine – you can be just as strong and healthy as people who eat meat. You do need to think carefully about what you eat, though. Try to make sure that your diet contains a mixture of different protein-rich foods such as lentils, pulses, nuts and soya. Dairy products like cheese and milk are also good protein sources for vegetarians.

Vitamins, Minerals and Fibre

Your body only needs tiny amounts of vitamins and minerals, but they are essential to keep you fit and healthy. They are found in many different foods, but fruits and vegetables are some of the best sources. Most doctors think we should try to eat five portions of fresh fruits and vegetables every day.

Vitamins

There are fifteen main vitamins, each of which is needed to maintain a healthy body. The table below shows some vitamins, the foods that provide them, and why the vitamins are needed.

Lack of particular vitamins can cause health problems. For example, rickets is caused by lack of Vitamin D. In people with rickets, bones cannot form properly and are weak and bendy.

Eating an orange will give you plenty of Vitamin C.

Vitamin	Good sources	Needed for
A	dairy products, eggs and green vegetables	healthy eyes and skin
B (there are several different B vitamins)	wholemeal bread, meat, liver and some beans	healthy skin and general good health
C	citrus fruits and green vegetables	healing cuts and strengthening your body's defences
D	oily fish and dairy products	strong teeth and bones

Dairy products like these are rich in calcium, which helps to build strong bones and teeth.

Minerals

Minerals are another group of chemicals that your body needs to stay healthy. There are about twenty minerals that are essential to your body. Two of the most important are iron and calcium.

Foods that are rich in iron include meat, eggs, liver and leafy green vegetables. Your body needs iron to make a protein called haemoglobin. This forms part of the blood that carries oxygen around your body. Lack of iron can cause an illness called anaemia, which makes you feel tired and unwell.

Calcium is found in dairy products. It is part of the material that bones and teeth are made from. Without calcium, bones become weak and brittle. Many elderly people suffer from osteoporosis, which can be caused by a lack of calcium. Their bones become painful and break easily.

Fibre

Fibre is found in fruits and vegetables. It does not contain any nutrients for your body to absorb and use, but it is an important part of your diet. Fibre is bulky and helps food to move easily through the intestines. Most doctors think that including plenty of fibre in your diet can help to prevent illnesses such as bowel cancer.

Case notes

Can oranges really stop me getting a cold?

Many people eat oranges and drink orange juice to prevent them from catching colds. This will not stop you ever catching a cold again, but it can help to strengthen your body's own defences. Oranges, and other citrus fruit like grapefruit and lemons, contain a lot of Vitamin C, which helps your body to fight off colds and other germs.

Carbohydrates

Starches and sugars belong to a group of chemicals called carbohydrates. They provide energy and are found in a lot of the foods that we eat.

Starches

Foods that contain starch are good at making you feel full. Starchy foods include bread, pasta, rice and cereals. Some vegetables, like potatoes, are also good sources of starch. These foods provide energy, but they are not bad for your teeth. Also, as your body can only digest them slowly, you feel full for a long time and so it is easy to control how much you eat. Many doctors think that starchy foods should make up about two-fifths of our diet.

Cereal crops like this are ground into flour to make foods such as bread and pasta.

Sweets like these are delicious, but you should try not to eat too many!

Sugars

Sugars make foods taste sweet, and are found in foods such as cakes, biscuits, sweets and fizzy drinks. They are delicious and it can be very tempting to eat a lot of them! You should be careful not to eat too many sugary foods, though, as they are very bad for your teeth.

Also, a small portion of sugary food can provide a lot of energy, so it is easy to eat more than your body needs without realizing it. Sugary foods and drinks can give you a quick burst of energy just when you need it, but they do not satisfy you for very long. It makes sense to think of these foods as a treat – enjoy them once in a while, but try not to have them at every meal.

Some people find it difficult not to eat sugary foods because they really like the sweet taste. They may use artificial sweeteners instead. These are chemicals that make things taste sweet, as sugar does, but contain very little energy. Diet drinks are also sweetened with artificial sweeteners instead of sugar.

Case notes

Why is wholemeal bread better than white?

Bread is made from cereal grains such as wheat. These are full of vitamins and fibre. The grains are ground and turned into flour. All the grain is used to make wholemeal flour, so bread made from this contains a lot of vitamins and fibre.

To make white bread, a lot of the grain is thrown away, so the vitamins and fibre are lost. Flour for white bread has also often been through chemical processes such as bleaching to make it really white. So, it makes sense to eat wholemeal bread and get all those vitamins!

Fats and Oils

Fats and oils are found in fried foods, and also in many other foods such as dairy products and nuts. They are an important part of our diet because they provide a lot of energy as well as other important chemicals that our bodies need. Fats also help to keep your body warm.

There are two types of fat: saturated and unsaturated. Saturated fats are found in foods that come from animals, including dairy products and fatty meat. Unsaturated fats are found in non-animal foods like nuts and vegetable oils.

You can check how much fat a food contains by looking at the label.

INGREDIENTS AS SERVED (Greatest first)

Rice, Water, Beef, Prepared Soya Protein, Onion, Cornflour, Red & Green Peppers, Tomato, Sugar, Carrot, Peas, Beef Fat with Antioxidant (BHA), Curry Spices, Salt, Yeast Extract, Citric Acid, Flavour Enhancers (Monosodium Glutamate, Sodium 5'-Ribonucleotide), Colour (Caramel), Maltodextrin, Hydrogenated Vegetable Oil and Acidity Regulator (Sodium Citrate). Less than 10% meat as served.

NUTRITIONAL INFORMATION

Typical Values	Per 100g as Sold	Per 100g as Served
Energy	1526kJ / 365kcal	458kJ / 109kcal
Protein	11.5g	3.5g
Carbohydrate	63.7g	19.1g
of which Sugars	7.4g	2.2g
Fat	7.1g	2.1g
of which Saturates	3.3g	1.0g
Sodium	1.4g	0.4g
Fibre	5.2g	1.6g

Many doctors think that unsaturated fats are better for your health than saturated fats.

People from Mediterranean countries such as France and Italy cook food in plant oils like olive oil. In these countries, heart disease is less common. In many other countries, people cook their food in animal fats like lard. Here, heart disease is much more common. There may be other factors involved too, but doctors think that eating a lot of animal fat may increase a person's risk of suffering from heart problems.

Biscuits, cakes and sweet, buttery popcorn contain a lot of fat.

Many people try to avoid eating too much animal fat by choosing low-fat or fat-free options. Semi-skimmed milk is treated to remove some of the fat, and skimmed milk has all the fat removed. Yoghurt, cheese and ice cream made from semi-skimmed or skimmed milk contain less fat than those made from ordinary milk.

Some food producers have started to make low-fat versions of foods like cakes, biscuits and ready-made meals. These can all help people to eat the foods that they enjoy while reducing the amount of animal fat they are taking in.

Case notes

Why are fatty foods linked to heart disease?

A lot of scientific evidence suggests that eating a diet of fatty foods can lead to heart disease. This is because fatty foods contain chemicals that can clog up the blood vessels, making it difficult for blood to get through them. The heart has to pump harder to push the blood around the body, putting it under a lot of strain. Also, eating a lot of fatty food can make you overweight, and this again forces the heart to work harder.

Glossary

absorb	Soak up.
amino acid	One of the tiny units that proteins are made from.
anus	The opening through which faeces leaves the body.
bacteria	A type of micro-organism.
balanced diet	A selection of foods that contains all the nutrients needed to maintain health and fitness.
bladder	The organ where urine is stored until you go to the toilet.
canine	A pointed tooth at the side of the mouth.
carbohydrate	A type of nutrient that provides energy.
digestion	The process of breaking food into separate chemicals.
digestive system	The organs that together carry out the process of digestion.
enzyme	A chemical that helps chemical changes to take place.
faeces	Solid waste.
fibre	Plant material that helps food move easily through the intestines.
gall bladder	A pouch where bile is stored.
glucagon	A chemical involved in controlling the sugar level in blood.
incisor	A sharp tooth at the front of the mouth.

insulin	A chemical involved in controlling the sugar level in blood.
kidneys	Organs that filter the blood.
large intestine	Part of the digestive system where water is absorbed.
liver	An organ involved in many chemical changes in the body.
mineral	A substance needed in very small quantities to maintain health.
molar	A large, strong tooth at the back of the mouth.
nutrients	The parts of your food that your body can use.
pancreas	The organ that produces insulin and glucagon.
protein	A nutrient that is needed for growth and repair.
rectum	The end of the large intestine, where faeces is stored until you go to the toilet.
saliva	A liquid that softens food in the mouth.
salivary glands	The parts of the mouth that produce saliva.
small intestine	Part of the digestive system where nutrients are absorbed.
stomach	The organ where food is broken down into chyme.
urine	Liquid waste.
vitamin	A substance needed in very small quantities to maintain health.

Further Information

Books

The Oxford Children's A to Z of the Human Body by Bridget and Neil Ardley (Oxford University Press, 2003)

Usborne Internet-Linked Complete Book of the Human Body by Anna Claybourne (Usborne Publishing, 2003)

DK Guide to the Human Body (Dorling Kindersley, 2004)

My Healthy Body: Digestion by Jen Green (Franklin Watts, 2003)

Look at Your Body: Digestion by Steve Parker (Franklin Watts, 2001)

Under the Microscope: Digesting by Angela Royston (Franklin Watts, 2001)

Websites

www.innerbody.com
click on picture of digestive system

www.brainpop.com/health/index
click on "digestive system"

www.kidshealth.org/teen/nutrition

Index